Left fielder Garret Anderson

THE STORY OF THE LOS ANGELES ANGELS

Third baseman Anthony Rendon

THE STORY OF THE

LOS ANGELES ANGELS

JIM WHITING

Outfielder Mike Trout

CREATIVE EDUCATION / CREATIVE PAPERBACKS

Published by Creative Education and Creative Paperbacks
P.O. Box 227, Mankato, Minnesota 56002
Creative Education and Creative Paperbacks are imprints of
The Creative Company
www.thecreativecompany.us

Book Design by Graham Morgan
Art direction by Blue Design (www.bluedes.com)

Images by Alamy Stock Photo/Cal Sport Media, 31; Associated Press/AMY SANCETTA, 20, Brandon Sloter/Icon Sportswire, cover; Getty Images/Al Bello, 6 (top, left), Chris Bernacchi/Diamond Images, 30, Daniel Shirey, 2, Diamond Images, 6 (bottom, right), 15, 18, DON EMMERT, 9, Focus On Sport, 6 (bottom, left), George Kubas/Diamond Images, 29, Harry How, 6 (top, right), 10, Jed Jacobsohn, 1, Jeff Gross, 7 (bottom, right), 11, John Sleezer/Kansas City Star, 3, 25, Leon Halip, 4–5, 32, MCT, 26–27, Rob Leiter, 19, Rogers Photo Archive, 12, Scott Boehm, 7 (top, right), 22–23, Stephen Dunn, 7 (top, left), V.J. Lovero, cover, 16, Walter Iooss Jr., 7 (bottom, left); Wikimedia Commons/Richard Anderson (Rich Anderson), 10

Library of Congress Cataloging-in-Publication Data
Names: Whiting, Jim, 1943- author
Title: The story of the Los Angeles Angels / by Jim Whiting.
Description: Mankato, Minnesota : Creative Education and Creative Paperbacks, [2026] | Series: Creative sports: Major League Baseball | Includes index. | Audience: Ages 8-12 | Audience: Grades 4-6 | Summary: "Discover the Los Angeles Angels' thrilling journey from underdogs to champions, featuring iconic players, historic victories, and the Major League Baseball team's unforgettable moments. Written for middle-grade readers. Includes table of contents, sidebars, and index"– Provided by publisher.
Identifiers: LCCN 2025013114 (print) | LCCN 2025013115 (ebook) | ISBN 9798895810965 library binding | ISBN 9798896800491 paperback | ISBN 9798895812228 ebook
Subjects: LCSH: Los Angeles Angels (Baseball team)–History–Juvenile literature
Classification: LCC GV875.A6 W55 2026 (print) | LCC GV875.A6 (ebook)
LC record available at https://lccn.loc.gov/2025013114
LC ebook record available at https://lccn.loc.gov/2025013115

Printed in the United States

Pitcher Jered Weaver

ANGELS

CONTENTS

EXTRA INNINGS

A MIRACLE COMEBACK

In more than 40 years of existence, the Anaheim Angels (later the Los Angeles Angels) of Major League Baseball (MLB) had not enjoyed much success. Since 1961, they had made the playoffs just three times. They lost each time.

That changed in 2002. The Angels won 99 games. They finally won a playoff series, defeating the New York Yankees in the American League Division Series (ALDS), three games to one. Then the team easily swept aside the Minnesota Twins in the American League Championship Series (ALCS).

Now they faced the San Francisco Giants in the World Series. The Giants eked out a 4–3 win in Game 1. Anaheim came back to tie the series with a wild 11–10 victory in Game 2. Their bats stayed hot in Game 3 as they cruised to a 10–4 win. The Giants had another 4–3 win in Game 4. They pounded the Angels in Game 5, 16–4. The Giants only needed one more win to take the Series.

It looked like the Giants would get that win in Game 6. San Francisco led 5–0 as the Angels came to bat in the bottom of the seventh inning. Up to that point, they had just two singles. With one out, third baseman Troy Glaus singled. Designated hitter Brad Fullmer also

Third baseman Troy Glaus

DARIN ERSTAD
OUTFIELD/FIRST BASE
ANGELS SEASONS: 1996–2006
HEIGHT: 6-FOOT-2
WEIGHT: 195 POUNDS
KEY STATS: .286 BATTING AVERAGE, 114 HOME RUNS, 625 RBIS, 2X ALL-STAR

MAN OF MANY TALENTS

In high school, Darin Erstad was an exceptional athlete. He played football and hockey, won state titles in track and field, and batted .492 in baseball. He was an obvious selection as North Dakota Athlete of the Year in 1992. Erstad played college baseball at the University of Nebraska, where he set a school record with 261 career hits. The Angels made him the top overall choice in the 1995 MLB Draft. He led MLB in 2000 with 240 hits. He especially excelled in the field, winning three Gold Glove awards. He became the first player to win the award at two different positions: outfield in 2000 and 2002, and first base in 2004.

singled. First baseman Scott Spezio brought the fans in Edison International Field of Anaheim to their feet with a long home run. "That was far and away the biggest hit of our whole season," said center fielder Darin Erstad. Reliever Brendan Donnelly pitched a scoreless top of the eighth.

Erstad did his part to keep the fans excited with a home run to lead off the bottom of the eighth. That brought Anaheim to within a single run at 5–4. It was especially remarkable because Erstad was playing without knowing he had a broken hand. Pinch hitter Chone Figgins singled. Left fielder Garret Anderson dropped a pop fly into short left field for another single.

On a 2–1 pitch, Glaus sent a long fly ball into deep left-center field for a double that plated both Figgins and Anderson. The Angels took the lead, 6–5!

Ace reliever Troy Percival struck out the first Giants batter. The next one fouled out. Percival struck out the third batter. The Angels won Game 6 to tie the series!

"To be able to come back from the five down, probably 99 percent of the people out there thought we had no chance," Glaus said. "But the 25 or 30 guys in our dugout thought we'd be all right."

In Game 7, Anderson hit a three-run double in the third inning. Anaheim held on to topple the Giants, 4–1. After 42 years, the Angels had won the World Series the first time they appeared! "These fans have been waiting a long, long time for this," Glaus said. "And I know we're all happy to be part of the team to bring it to them."

LOS ANGELE
SANGE
EL

STAR-STUDDED START

The American League (AL) was founded in 1901 with eight teams. In 1960, the league decided to add two more teams. One was the Washington Senators. (Later, they became the Texas Rangers.) The second team would be located in Los Angeles. Cowboy singing star and movie actor Gene Autry was the new team's owner. He named it the Angels. The name recognized the Los Angeles Angels team in the minor Pacific Coast League from 1903 to 1957. The new MLB team was nicknamed the Halos because their first logo had a halo around the top of the "A."

The Angels began play in 1961. The team's temporary home was Wrigley Field in Los Angeles. Its short fences made it a hitter's paradise. Teams combined to hit 248 home runs at Wrigley Field that season. It was an MLB record that stood for 35 years. The Angels won 46 games at home. But they managed only 24 wins on the road.

The following year, the Angels moved to Dodger Stadium. They finished with an 86–76 record. The season highlight was a no-hitter by rookie pitcher Bo Belinsky. In an odd coincidence, Belinsky was the losing pitcher when the Angels were on the receiving end of a no-hitter later that season. They dropped to 70–91 in 1963.

In 1964, pitcher Dean Chance accounted for 20 of the team's 82 wins. Just 23 years old, he became the youngest Cy Young Award winner in history. Meanwhile, 22-year-old shortstop Jim Fregosi batted .277. He smacked 18 homers and 72 runs batted in (RBIs). Fregosi teamed up with second baseman Bobby Knoop to form one of the league's best double-play combinations.

Pitchers Ken McBride, Dean Chance, and Bo Belinsky

In 1965, the team changed their name to the California Angels. The following season, the Angels moved to nearby Anaheim. They settled into the brand-new Anaheim Stadium. Attendance nearly tripled. But the Angels continued to miss the postseason. In 1969, the AL split into two divisions. The Angels were in the West Division. They posted an 86–76 record in 1970. It still was not good enough for the playoffs. Management decided to make a change. They traded fan-favorite Fregosi to the New York Mets before the 1972 season. In return, they received pitcher Nolan Ryan. With the Mets, Ryan had struggled to control his pitches and had limited playing time. The trade transformed his career. He learned to control his wicked fastball. In 1973, Ryan struck out a MLB-leading 383 batters. He also threw the first two of his seven career no-hitters.

Despite Ryan's success, the team continued to struggle. It finally posted a winning record in 1978 and tied for second in the AL West. Still, almost two decades into their existence, the Angels had yet to play in the postseason.

A TASTE OF SUCCESS

Fregosi ended his MLB playing career in June 1978. Autry hired him as manager the next day. In 1979, the Angels led the major leagues with 866 runs. They won their first-ever AL West championship. Veterans such as first baseman Rod Carew, second baseman Bobby Grich, and right fielder Dan Ford had fine seasons. Designated hitter Don Baylor topped the major leagues with 139 RBIs and 120 runs scored. He was named AL Most Valuable Player (MVP). "Every day I went to the park, I knew I'd get two or three hits and some RBIs," Baylor

JIM FREGOSI
SHORTSTOP/MANAGER
ANGELS SEASONS: 1961–71 AS PLAYER, 1978–81 AS MANAGER
HEIGHT: 6-FOOT-1
WEIGHT: 190 POUNDS
KEY STATS: .268 BATTING AVERAGE, 115 HOME RUNS, 546 RBIS, 6X ALL-STAR

EXPERT CYCLIST

On May 20, 1968, the Angels hosted the Boston Red Sox. Jim Fregosi hit a reverse cycle. That means he hit a home run, a triple, a double, and a single in that order in the same game. Fregosi swatted a solo round-tripper in the first inning. Two innings later, he ripped a triple. He grounded out in the fifth. He doubled to right field in the eighth. In the ninth, the score was tied. Fregosi was walked intentionally. The game went into extra innings. Fregosi came up to bat in the bottom of the 11th. A runner was on second. Fregosi completed the cycle with a game-winning single. It was just the seventh reverse cycle in MLB history.

First base/designated hitter Rod Carew

ROD CAREW
FIRST BASE/DESIGNATED HITTER
ANGELS SEASONS: 1979–85
HEIGHT: 6-FOOT-0
WEIGHT: 170 POUNDS
KEY STATS: .314 BATTING AVERAGE, 74 HOME RUNS, 733 RBIS, 6X ALL-STAR

LEARNING DISCIPLINE

During his MLB career with the Minnesota Twins and the Angels, Rod Carew became one of just 33 players with 3,000 hits. He credits his six years in the U.S. Marine Corp Reserves with the feat. "When I first came up to the big leagues in 1967, I was a little bit of a hothead," he said. "But after two weeks of war games [with the Marines] every summer, I realized that baseball was not do-or-die. That kind of discipline made me the player I became." He was a 12-time All-Star with the Twins. When he joined the Angels, the team made him the highest-paid MLB player at the time with an $800,000 contract. He added six more All-Star nods with the Angels before retiring. To honor him, the American League batting title was renamed the Rod Carew American League batting title in 2016.

explained. The Angels squared off against the Baltimore Orioles in the ALCS. It was their first trip to the postseason. But Baltimore won, three games to one.

The Angels wanted more. But Ryan left the team before the 1980 season. Baylor was hurt. The Angels finished with a disappointing 65–95 record. The following season, shortened by a players' strike, was only slightly more successful.

The 1982 Angels team was "made up of veterans with sore muscles, with tired arms, with drained emotions," Grich said. But Baylor was healthy again. Left fielder Brian Downing blossomed. In his first year with the Angels, right fielder Reggie Jackson led the majors with 39 home runs.

The team racked up 93 wins. It won the AL West. The Angels faced the Milwaukee Brewers in the ALCS. California won the first two games. It looked like the team was on its way to the World Series. But the Brewers won the next three games. The Angels were out.

A disappointing 70–92 season followed that defeat. Things were better in 1984. The team finished just three victories shy of the AL West title. On September 17, Jackson smacked his 500th career home run. Thirteen days later, Mike Witt pitched a perfect game. In 1985, four players pounded 20 or more home runs. The Angels finished the season only one game behind the division-winning Kansas City Royals.

California compiled 92 victories and topped the AL West in 1986. They met the Boston Red Sox in the ALCS. The Angels won three of the first four games. It looked as if they had the series locked in Game 5. They entered the ninth inning with a 5–2 lead. But they could not hold on. The Angels

Designated hitter Don Baylor

lost the next two games as well. It would be a long time before they would see the postseason again.

HAPPY HALOS

The Angels recaptured some of their swagger in 1989. They stayed in contention for most of the season. But following a six-game losing streak in late September, the team was out of the playoff chase.

California failed to muster a winning record in the next five seasons. Right fielder Tim Salmon provided a rare bright spot in those dull seasons. He was named Rookie of the Year in 1993. Two years later, California led the AL West for much of the season. Salmon, center fielder Jim Edmonds, and left fielder Garret Anderson gave the Halos one of the best

Right fielder Tim Salmon

TIM SALMON
RIGHT FIELD/DESIGNATED HITTER
ANGELS SEASONS: 1992–2004, 2006
HEIGHT: 6-FOOT-3
WEIGHT: 200 POUNDS
KEY STATS: .265 BATTING AVERAGE, 299 HOME RUNS, 1,016 RBIS, ROOKIE OF THE YEAR 1993

FISH STORY 1

Tim Salmon was just 17 when the Atlanta Braves drafted him in the 18th round of the 1986 MLB Draft. He chose to attend Grand Canyon University instead. The move paid off. "Our coaches demanded a nose-to-the-grindstone work ethic," he said. "It was the perfect environment for me to develop my God-given baseball skills." Three years later, the Angels chose him in the third round of the 1989 draft. After playing briefly at the end of the 1992 season, Salmon moved into the starting lineup in 1993. It was the start of a heavenly career. He slammed 31 home runs and had 95 RBIs to earn Rookie of the Year honors. He went on to play his entire career with the Angels and become a fan favorite, nicknamed "King Fish" and "Mr. Angel." He was also known as "Slammin' Salmon" because his 299 home runs were the most in team history until 2020.

outfields in MLB. By August 1, they had a commanding 11-game lead in the division. Then, the Angels collapsed. They finished the season tied with the Seattle Mariners. The teams met in a one-game playoff. Seattle won, 9–1. "We were the best team for three months," shortstop Gary DiSarcina said. "But you've got to be the best team when it counts."

After a sub-par 1996, the team changed its name again. It became the Anaheim Angels. The roster of young players matured. The pitching staff flourished behind intimidating save specialist Troy Percival. The Angels picked up speed in the next few years.

The final pieces of the puzzle started coming together in 2000. Third baseman Troy Glaus, who had joined the Angels in 1998, developed into a power hitter. He led the league with 47 home runs. He slugged 41 in 2001.

On April 23, 2002, Anaheim's record was 6–14. Five days later, shortstop David Eckstein hit a grand slam. The following day, he hit another grand slam, giving the Angels a walk-off win. The team pounded the Cleveland Indians, 21–2. The Angels had a new spark.

That spark became a flame that carried the team to the playoffs for the first time in 16 years. They advanced to the World Series for the first time. They staged the miracle comeback in Game 6 and cruised to victory in Game 7.

The Angels slumped to 77–85 in 2003. During the season, businessman Arte Moreno bought the team. He immediately began spending money to improve it. In both 2004 and 2005, Anaheim captured the AL West crown. Powering the team were such newcomers as slugging right fielder Vladimir Guerrero and burly pitcher Bartolo Colón. The Angels fell to the eventual world champions both times—the Red Sox in the 2004 ALDS, and the Chicago White Sox in

Pitcher Jered Weaver

the 2005 ALCS. Between those seasons, the team changed its name to Los Angeles Angels of Anaheim.

The Halos were hungry for more. "We think we have the makings of a pretty good ballclub," general manager Bill Stoneman said before the 2007 season. He was right. The Angels quickly gained the division lead. But they could not overcome the surging Red Sox in the ALDS. Boston swept the Angels in three games.

The disappointing finish only fueled the Angels' fire. In 2008, the team won 13 of its last 18 games. It finished with a whopping 100 victories. That is the best record in team history. Once again, however, the Red Sox shot down the high-flying Angels in the ALDS.

TWO SUPERSTARS COME OUT

Los Angeles took revenge in 2009. It swept the Red Sox in the ALDS. Then the team headed to New York, where it faced the Yankees in the ALCS. New York prevailed in six games. The following year, the Angels tumbled to 80–82. It was their first losing record in seven seasons.

They rebounded to 86–76 in 2011. The team's first draft choice in 2009, Mike Trout, had two brief stints with Los Angeles that year. The outfielder was not an instant sensation. But pitcher Dan Haren saw signs of his greatness. "There was never a point even with his early struggles that any of us thought that he wasn't legit."

Trout was certainly "legit" in 2012. He became the first player in MLB history to rack up 30 home runs, 45 stolen bases, and 125 runs in a single season.

Outfielder Mike Trout

MIKE TROUT
OUTFIELDER
ANGELS SEASONS: 2011–PRESENT
HEIGHT: 6-FOOT-2
WEIGHT: 235 POUNDS
KEY STATS: .299 BATTING AVERAGE, 378 HOME RUNS, 954 RBIS, 11X ALL-STAR

FISH STORY 2

The Angels wanted to take Mike Trout with their first pick in the 2009 MLB Draft. But they only had the 25th pick. They were afraid that he would be gone by then. Legendary Oakland Athletics general manager Billy Beane had scouted Trout personally. Fortunately, Beane and the other general managers passed on Trout. He became the Angels' best-ever draft pick. In 2019, *Baseball America* called him the best current player in MLB. Trout displayed a unique combination of power, speed, and baseball smarts. Through 2024, he was an 11-time All-Star. He has been named Most Valuable Player (MVP) three times. Only Barry Bonds has more MVP awards. The team gave him a 12-year contract extension in 2019 worth more than $428 million. It was the richest contract in North American professional sports history.

He was a unanimous choice as Rookie of the Year. Los Angeles also added slugging first baseman Albert Pujols. He drove in 105 runs. But even with its new stars, the team missed the postseason. Two years later, Trout enjoyed his first MVP season. His play propelled the Angels to the AL West title. But the Royals swept them in the ALDS.

Following the 2015 season, the team name was shortened to Los Angeles Angels. Despite Trout's second MVP performance, the Angels won only 74 games in 2016. They finished the following season at 80–82. They had the same record in 2018. One highlight was signing Japanese superstar Shohei Ohtani. He was a baseball rarity—an outstanding pitcher and a deadly hitter. He was named Rookie of the Year. But the struggles continued in 2019 as the team dropped to 72–90. Although Trout picked up his third MVP award, injuries to Ohtani and other key players figured into the decline. No pitcher won more than eight games.

The team finished 26–34 in the 2020 season, which was shortened due to the COVID-19 pandemic. They didn't qualify for an eight-team tournament to determine the overall league winner.

In 2021, Ohtani smashed 46 home runs. He also won nine games on the mound. He was named AL MVP. But the team finished under .500 again, with a 77–85 record. The 2022 season was almost the same, with the team at 73–85.

Ohtani hit 46 home runs again in 2023 and had 10 wins. Once again he was named MVP. But Los Angeles could only match the previous season's mark.

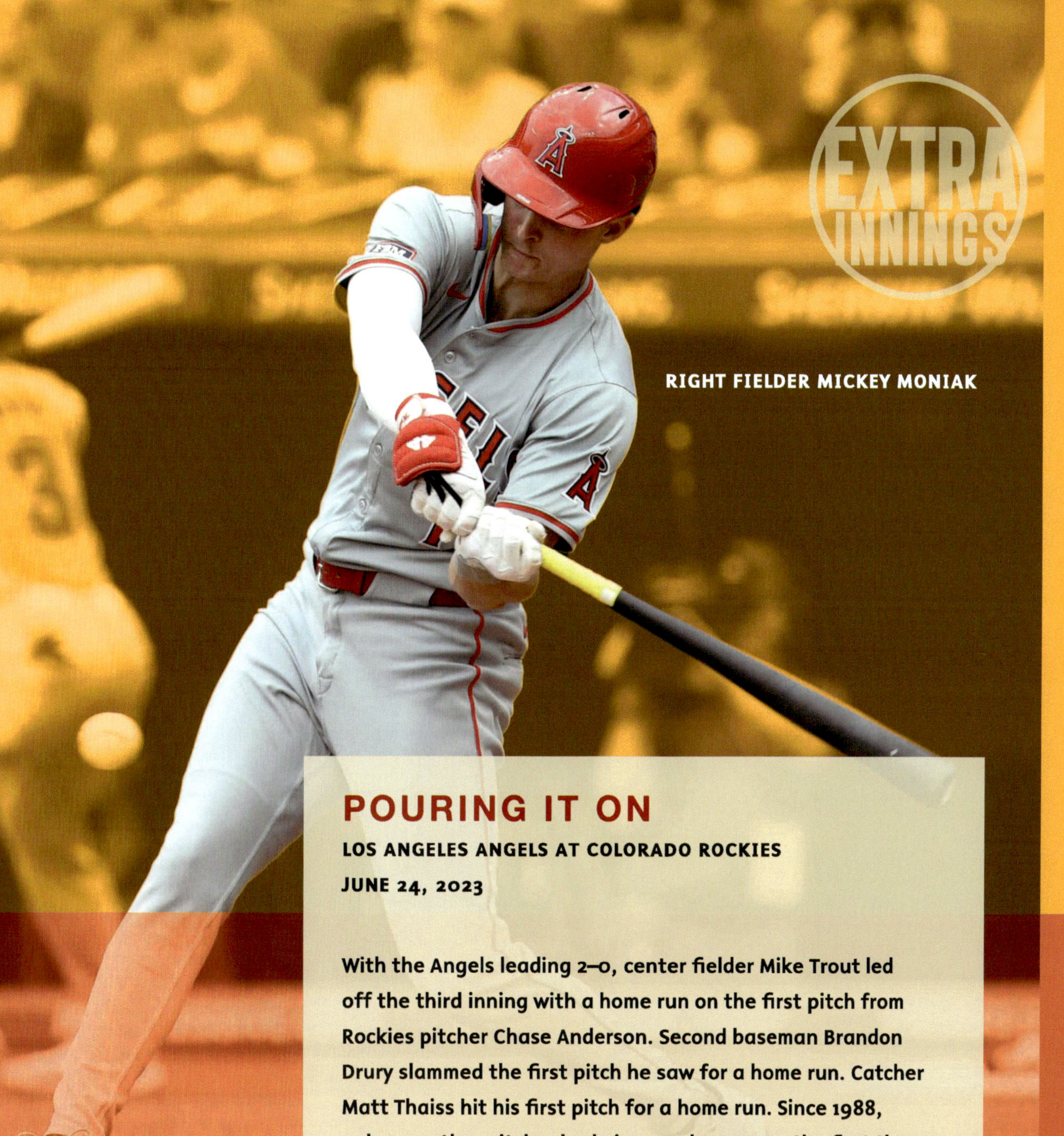

RIGHT FIELDER MICKEY MONIAK

POURING IT ON

LOS ANGELES ANGELS AT COLORADO ROCKIES

JUNE 24, 2023

With the Angels leading 2–0, center fielder Mike Trout led off the third inning with a home run on the first pitch from Rockies pitcher Chase Anderson. Second baseman Brandon Drury slammed the first pitch he saw for a home run. Catcher Matt Thaiss hit his first pitch for a home run. Since 1988, only one other pitcher had given up homers on the first three pitches of an inning. The Angels tacked on 10 more runs in the inning for a total of 13. They followed that up with eight more in the fourth inning. They added single tallies in the sixth and eighth innings. A late Colorado home run made the final score 25–1. That is the Angels franchise record for runs in a game! "Today was just one of those days, where everyone was feeling good and we were getting the right pitches to hit," said right fielder Mickey Moniak. He was one of two Angels with five hits.

ANGELS
16

Designated hitter/pitcher Shohei Ohtani

Ohtani became a free agent after the season. He didn't have far to go. He joined the Los Angeles Dodgers, where he picked up his third MVP award.

Ohtani wasn't the only loss. Trout missed most of the 2024 season with injuries. Without them, the Angels tumbled to a 63–99 mark. It was the worst full-season record in franchise history. There was one consolation. The Angels remained the only MLB team without a 100-loss season.

The Angels have spent decades entertaining fans on the West Coast. Despite recent losses, they fly on. Fans have every reason to believe that the Halos will soon encircle another World Series trophy.

Pitcher Yusei Kikuchi

INDEX